'THE BOSS'

Written by

Hency Anthony Bunner

How the Boss may try to

Control Employees

TABLE OF CONTENT

INTRODUCTION

This book is being written for all of us out there that do not like our jobs and do not know why. When you encounter a person or situation that upsets you, you must ask yourself why? Chances are that person is playing or tampering with your self-esteem. Self-esteem is simply how you feel about yourself. Some bosses and fellow employees have developed an ability to make others feel unimportant. The trick is to recognize what is happening at the time.

So, let us peel back the outer layer of some of these people and see exactly how they do it; so that it is easier to understand all the tricks. I have invented an individual called 'The Boss'. 'The Boss' is really a composite of about 20 individuals I've met over my last 30 years in business plus stories given to me by other executives in business. 'The Boss' is the type of person you love to hate.

When the Boss was a little boy, he must have tried pulling the wings out of butterflies and then watched them suffer. He has no mercy, empathy, or regret. He will eliminate anyone who gets in his way by whatever means possible.

The Boss has control by:

- Creating an image of himself as being superior to everyone. Creating rules and decisions in his favor.
- Controlling communications through letters, memo & meetings. Shuttle manipulation over conversations.
- Downright dirty tricks and intimidation.
- Finally, getting employees fired that he does not like.

As you read about 'The Boss', you will find yourself chuckling because it reminds you of a person or situation that happened to you or a friend. Although I have written this book to be humorous, do not kid yourself, when someone pulls these tricks, someone gets hurt or fired.

Before we get started, I would like to explain that several of the stories in this book have been given to me by men & women in business who have suffered under 'The Boss'. I would like to thank all of you for your contributions to this book. As you read the book you may associate with your stories written as I promised

YOU'RE FIRED

Most people fear being fired more than any other thing in life. Getting fired is the loss of income. It is a statement that you have not worked to the full satisfaction of your employer. It means the loss of friends you have made over the years at work. Getting fired means admitting to your family and friends you have failed. If you have done your job and your boss still does not like you, you are gone. Most bosses do not want to fire you. They want you too quiet. That way they do not have to pay you unemployment or benefits. So, they create an atmosphere of discomfort. Here are a few dirty tricks your boss can pull on you:

- Find mistakes and make you correct them repeatedly.
- Find personal fault and criticize in public.
- Find something you do not like doing and make you do it.
- Cut your budget, support team, expenses, etc.
- Nit-pick your expense account, explain & have receipts on everything.
- Force you to increase performance.
- Make you work overtime without pay.
- Make you work weekends.
- Create unreasonable deadlines.

- Give you meaningless assignments that go nowhere.
- Create confusion by constantly changing goals and objectives.
- Assign you projects you are not qualified for and then make you responsible.
- Keep you in the dark on major decisions.
- Never give you a raise, cut your pay and bonuses
- Transfer you to a place you do not want to live.
- Everything you do must be in writing and approved.
- Keep telling upper management you are incompetent.
- Reassign your workload to your future replacement.

The mushroom theory is "keep you in the dark, feed you a lot of shit and when you are fully grown, cut you off at the knees". If you see any of these tactics coming, get your resume updated because the light at the end of the tunnel is a train.

YOU'RE NOBODY

Ever notice when someone wants something from you, you are the most important person in the world? After they get what they want, they do not care who the hell you are. Or the opposite, if you have nothing to give them, they do not give a dam about you.

Good examples are politicians. During the election period, these guys are knocking on your door, kissing your babies, and shaking hands. They act like they are your best friend. They promise to work their ass off for you when they get in office. Once they are in office, they are gone. Ever try to call them? Right, you cannot get through. They build a communications wall around them that you cannot penetrate.

This isolation also applies to upper management and workers, rich and poor, social élite and the low class, senators /congressmen and constituents, sports figures and fans, pop stars and fans, even the Pope and his subjects, etc. Once they get what they want and have your money, they do not give a rat's ass about you. These people will isolate themselves in the fear of some nut trying to harm them. The further away they get from the people who put them there, the more they forget their real purpose, serve the people. The power, greed and control set in. It is like an intoxicating drug they cannot give up.

If you want to take away someone power, do not vote for a politician, do not go to concert or sporting event, buy a different product and anything else that will affect their income.

Here is the kicker. We forget, we all came into this world with nothing and we will go out with nothing. We own nothing; only get to use it while we are here. Money and power cannot buy you happiness. Money will only give you freedom. Power gets you people who want to take it away from you.

The most important people in your life are those that you give unconditional love, your family and close friends. Stay close to those who will give you the shirt off their back and never ask for anything in return. So, stay away from money sucking egotistical people that only want to use you for their own personal gain and then discard.

you. Do not give them credit they do not deserve. To some, if you are not somebody, you are nobody. To your family and friends, you are everything.

I MAKE THE CALLS – NOT YOU

- Make the exception not the rule.
- Make directions incomplete, confusing, unclear, or misleading. Screw it up the first time (you will not be asked to do it again)

- The perfect solution (if some else has the perfect solution, muck it up) Know all the rules (force other to obey even if it does not apply) Punish violators of the rules.
- Create the rules.
- The "What If" scenario
- Have the solution at hand when the problem occurs.
- Show others how to make the right decisions. Be a know it all. Create delays and then come up with the solution.
- Never give out enough information to solve the problem or complete the project.
- Call a meeting together for the smallest problems.
- Make everyone panic at every little problem. The world is coming to an end. Use "standard practices" book for the answers. Never make an exception.

- Set rules to be unrealistic or unobtainable then force others to comply. Give other objectives and then keep changing them.
- Encourage others to make decisions then reverse them. Never train your replacement.
- Take responsibility for an action, then do nothing.
- Leave the risky decision to someone else. Let them take the blame. Claim you are not part of the process; you are out of the circle.
- Give the same assignment to more than one person. Give out useless assignment that go nowhere.
- Never solve the problem. Go around in circles. Over analyze.

Destroy Your Employee's Self-Esteem

- Refuse to shake hands.
- Walk away while someone is talking.
- Tear up your employee's report in front of everyone.
- Never make statements, always ask questions.
- Use groups to gang up on one person. Look at others as thou they were stupid. The world is always coming to an end.
- Refuse to talk to someone that is less than

you.

- Make others prove it when you are wrong.
- Insult others in from of their associates.
- Make others wait.

    In the lobby

     While you are on the phone

   After work

     For meetings for lunch

- When in your office - just walk out
- Find fault with everything.
- Be insensitive to personal problems.
- Keep a person's job in jeopardy by threatening to fire them.
- Get angry or emotional for no reason.
- Keep changing your mind on issues. Keep others confused and defensive.
- When cornered, use subjective & illogical arguments. Always talk in "one upmanship" to others.
- Have an "I already know it" attitude.

- Always be the teacher. Show other how you can do it better.
- Correct mistakes of others in front of everyone.
- Tell others you do not appreciate the way they act.
- Criticize the person and not the act.
- Explain why a person will never be better than others.
- Play and win for only one team -
- Set others up to lose by not helping when they fail.
- Pretend you are in charge when you are not.
- Tell everyone you make the final decisions.
- Get others to complain about you to management so they look at you as troublemaker.
- Never forgive someone for a mistake.
- Keep bring it up the mistake over & over.

- Check all work done by subordinates.
- No one can even go to the bathroom without permission.
- Give the name of someone you want to get rid of to headhunters.
- Let others know when someone is looking for a new outside job.
- Call people at night, weekends, lunch, etc.
- Start rumors and lies about others. Make your secretary lie for you.
- When a subordinate succeeds, do not give any credit.
- When a goal is achieved, raise the goal.
- Go through waste baskets for information.
- Ease drops on conversations.
- Read others mail, faxes, etc. in the mail room early in the morning.
- Make others travel on their own time.
- Tell someone to lie for you.

- Never take the blame when something goes wrong.

- Never go on vacation when everyone else is working.

- Send someone on vacation. While they are gone, find fault with their work.

- Do not let subordinates talk to anyone over you.

- Steal ideas from others and use them for yourself.

FALSE IDOLS

Don't you just hate it when someone brags about themselves? It seems to be OK if someone else brags about you, but you cannot do it yourself. If someone else does it, it is pride. If you do it, it is arrogance. When you do it, you appear to be better. These people come across as being conceited, self-centered and egotistical. They are insecure people crying out for attention. They want to be important and no one is paying attention.

How do you feel with someone shuts you out, turns away, ignores you. You feel rejected and unwanted. In some cultures, it is a form of punishment called shunning. Shunning is when everyone turns their back on you and pretends you do not exist. Diminish our self-worth and we feel alone and unwanted. It emotionally hurts.

On the other hand, we have needs and create idols. Maybe yours is a performer, sports figure, someone with power, money or someone who is better than you? Idol do not exist, we create them. Your belief makes them famous. Once you stop believing, they are worthless and do not exist. Let me explain. Here is a story that changed my life. It was in my freshman year in college. A professor called Dr. Augustine was teaching a class in human relations. In his first class he held up a five-dollar bill. He asked, "What is this".

We answered, it is $5.00, money, used to buy things, payment of debt and if you had enough of it, it is wealth, power, fame, etc. Here is when our learned professor shocked all of us. He said, "It is only paper and ink and your belief in this paper and ink is what makes it valuable."

To this day, I have never forgotten that statement. It opened my mind to a new way of thinking. The concept did not only apply to a $5.00 bill but everyone and everything. More important I realized I had a new power. All people and things were important because I made them important. I could decide who or what was valuable not them. Once I stopped believing, they were worthless. So, who is included in your realm of people and things? The list is endless. The company you worked for, people in government, entertainment, sports, what you buy, where you go, even your faith. My vote, what I purchase, where I eat, travel, what I do in life are all part of my power.

I cannot say this loud enough, YOU HAVE THE POWER NOT THEM! Do not let anyone put false idols in front of you and expect you to believe. Once you look harder, you may find they are only paper and ink, skin and bone, smoke and mirrors trying to make you believe in something that maybe is worthless.

PERCEPTION VS REALITY

Perception is a word we use to describe how we look at life. Perception is reality. If you believe something to be true in your own mind, it is true. The word "believe" is used to accept something to be true even if it cannot be proven to be true. For example, do you believe in God? Have you ever seen God? Do you know if he/she really exists? But you still believe, therefore he/she exists. I do not want to debate your beliefs, just point out the concept of perception. Here is the hook, if I can get you to believe something to be true and you believe it to be true, I can control you. I can control how you live your life simply by programming your beliefs which have nothing to do with reality.

This happens a lot with companies. The company would like you to believe that they are the best. Isn't that what advertising being all about? For customers, it is called brand naming. For employees, it is called loyalty. You buy the product or work harder based on what the company has you believe to be true.

You have a right to your opinion. You act on this opinion based on what you believe. Don't you think it is strange that elections are won and lost by a few votes? Half of the population believes in one thing and the other believe something else. Who is right and who is wrong? My dad once said; never argue politics or religion because no one will win. It is all based on belief.

Take my beautiful and charming wife. When we first met, she did not like me. That happens a lot in first encounter relationships. Nine months later, we got married. What happened between our first encounter and getting married?

She was looking for the perfect relationship. She wanted someone who would give her security, respect, and admire her. She wanted someone who would care for her and put her number one in his life. I admit, I was a jerk when we first met, I told me. I wanted to impress her but that is not what she wanted. Even though I was all those things she wanted, her first perception was, this guy is a jerk. I had to change her mind. I had to change her perception. Once I came to my senses the rest was easy.

I have been in sales all my life. My objective in sales is to change your opinion on a product or service so you will buy.

You would be surprised at the number of tricks I have in my bag. The first thing I do is evaluate your motivations and fears. By the way, these tactics can be used on any relationship because they rely on your perception and not reality. The most powerful is fear. If you fear something and I convince you I have a way out, I can control you. OK, you have a mind of your own. Once you make up your mind, no one can change it. Want to make a bet? If you do not believe me, look at who you elect in government. Why do you believe one thing one day and something else the next? You change your mind all the time based on what others persuade you to believe. Once you understand how other people try to control your life, you can take control.

By the way, the last 21 years of marriage have been the best years of my life. Best sale I ever made.

YOU ARE STUPID

The reason I decided to write about other people thinking you are stupid came to me from a show I saw last night. A couple of guys from an advertising agency were having a drink at a bar. They just had made a presentation to a potential client. They were making fun of the competition because the opposing team had not gone to an Ivy League college. Surprise, not everyone who goes to Harvard is a genius or successful. The best education is the college of hard knocks. The

Romans had it right "experience is the best teacher".

Then there are people who do the "One ups men ship". Everything you say, they have done it better or know some who has. Before you can get your story out, they interrupt by saying how they did it already and did it better. I really feel sorry for these people who are crying out for attention. The worst thing you can do is get into a pissing match, the back and forth "One ups men ship" duel. Then you both become stupid.

I just love it when people talk you down because they know you do not understand the subject. I have run into people who try to better themselves by putting others down. It is unfortunate that some people can only increase their self-esteem by stepping on others.

Then there are those who keep in control by destroying your self-esteem because you might be advanced. They are afraid you will pass them by. This is pure jealousy. If they have control of your life, run.

How to counteract these guys is to pay no attention to them or run. If it is your boss, find another job. If it is a friend, find another friend.

If it is your spouse, get divorced. You are not going to change these people so get as far away from them as soon as possible. They will drag you down and destroy you.

PERFORMANCE REVIEW

If you have ever gone through a performance review you know how frightening it can be. You do not know if you will get a raise or get fired.

I believe the only reason management has performance reviews are to point out everything you have done wrong over the last year. The truth is they need an excuse not to give you a raise. You might have done a thousand things right and one ah-shit wipes them all out. Do not hope for a raise based on performance. It will never happen unless it is a cost-of-living raise.

My old boss started off by saying "can I see you in my office?" As soon as I heard those words, I knew it was bad news. If it were good news he would stay in my office.

To make the performance review even more uncomfortable, he would call me into his office when the sun was to his back and in my eye. His desk was higher than my chair so he could look down at me. To make things worse, he cut 3 inches off the front legs of my chair, so I kept sliding out. Also, my chair was made vinyl, so my back and pants got wet. He wanted me to sweat.

He must have taken notes on every little mistake throughout the year. After demoralizing me, he would then explain. He could not give me a raise because the company was not making money, or his budget was cut, or my performance was not up to par. Whatever the excuse, it was bull.

Then he would make the promises. The carrot and stick trick. This trick refers to a donkey and cart. The driver of a cart would tie a carrot to a stick and put it in front of the donkey.

When the donkey went forward after the carrot, the cart moved forward. In other words, no matter how hard the donkey tried, he was never going get that carrot. If that did not work, then diver would use a stick as punishment. My boss would say, if my performance improved and the company did better next year, then I had a good chance of getting a raise NEXT YEAR. On the other hand, if I did not perform, I would get fired. I guess he made an ass out of me.

One year I did get a raise and a new title. I was so proud I told all my friends. Later I realized I got sucker punched. My boss changed me form hourly to salary. I was enjoying the over time from working hourly, now my boss could work me evenings and weekends without paying me over time. The new title got me nothing. Boy, was I stupid.

CONTROL YOUR MEETINGS

- Take outside calling when in the meeting, then make everyone wait.
- Schedule the meeting for after work or weekends.
- Make the meeting longer than planned.
- Meet in your office and sit in position of control.
- Flooding the meeting with as many people as possible
- Polluting the meeting with nonessential people Only'
- Invite those you wish to control or can control.

- Give out results and not actions Assignments that go nowhere.

- Call meeting for no reason or purpose.

- Call meeting at a moment's notice.

- Make everything a project.

- Make double assignments.

- Call instant meeting Make everything a panic.

- Every meeting is an emergency.

- Be the only expert on the topic.

- Leave out people you can not to control.

- Put your back to the window.

- Sit at the head of the table.

- Come in late and sit in the back of the room.

- Sit at the back of the room and keep interrupting Use the black board to oversimplify.

- Up stage the speaker

- Get up and walk around the room when someone else is talking.

- Do not let others get a word in edgewise. Be pushy and forceful.

- Put others down or criticize them in front of others Take outside calls and messages.

- Have someone run out for more information, call in an outside expert to discredit someone.

- Take the minutes and then change them later.

- Makeup words.

- Talk over everyone's head Explain everything in baby talk!

- Keep interrupting.

- Fill your schedule with meeting so that are your never available.

- You can never be pulled out of a meeting.

- Use meeting to gang up on someone.

- Talk on subjects that you are an expert and no one else.

THE PAPER BAG THEORY

When I was younger, I got really frustrated trying to make money. My dad told me "You're trying to fight your way out of a paper bag". He saw a program on TV where a guy put boxing gloves on, then put in a human size paper bag and was challenged to the task of fighting his way out. Can you imagine this guy swinging at the bag from inside? Every time he took a swing the bag moved away. It was impossible for him to fight his way out. Does that sound familiar? Maybe that is how you feel about your life.

The paper bag is our life, and the boxing gloves are what are holding us back. The only way out is our will power, ambitions, talent, education, experience, finances, society, government, business opportunities and even religion. It is no wonder we cannot fight our way out. The cards are stacked against us before we even start.

Sometimes we did our own grave and we do not even know it. I run a sales and marketing company that helps find sales channels. A potential new client sent two of their best young marketing people to discuss how I could help their company. These guys were sharp, educated, talented and good looking. They had everything going for them.

Let me interject another quote from my dad "Pick your rut because you may have to stay in it for the rest of your life". So how does that apply to these two guys? I suggested to them with all their talent, they should go into business as partners and make a ton of money. A

blank look came over their faces. They said, "We can't".
They both had recently got married and both had a child
on the way. No way would they go home and tell their
wives they were quitting their jobs even if it was for
more money. Well, ladies, what would you do? These
guys knew exactly what their wives would do after all
the screaming. They picked the paper bag and the
gloves which they must live within. My dad was a coal
miner with a 4th grade education. He was very frustrated
with life and could not fight his way out of the paper
bag. After watching what he had gone through, I made
up my mind that I was not going to put on the gloves. I
was going to do everything possible to get out of that
bag. I was willing to claw and bite my way out. I had
inherited numerous fears and insecurities which did not
help. I was told to walk the line. I was told that I was not
as important as other people. Fortunately, one teacher
convinced me that I was smart enough to go to college.
That was the turning point. She showed me the way out
of the paper bag.

FEAR

If there is a cancer of the body, fear is the cancer of the mind. It can destroy your life as easily as the cancer that can attack your body. Once it starts and grows, it is exceedingly difficult to stop.

Fear was designed so that you would not harm yourself or anyone else. But when fear goes to extreme it can stop us from achieving wonderful things in life. Also, fear can be used by others to control and manipulate our lives.

So, what are you afraid of? Maybe it could be the loss a loved one, loss of your job and income, going to jail, even death. If you lose your job, who will make your house and car payments, pay your utility bills, feed your family, pay your doctor bills, educate your children, plan for retirement not counting vacations and entertainment?

I have put together a list of fears in the following pages. Go down the list and find which ones you are afraid of and ask yourself why. Ask yourself, who did this to you?

I am a dog lover. Occasionally I will put my hand out to a strange dog. Sometimes the dog will duck or shy away. The first thought that comes to mind is that dog was beat when it was a pup. The dog was trained to be afraid. Whoever did this was stupid, mean, or angry. Do not kid yourself;

people are trained the same way.

There are doctors that make a fortune trying to correct those fears. Once programmed, it is near impossible to change. Good old Woody Allan made funny movies about our fears and how they control our lives. But stopping us from the enjoyment of life is no laughing matter.

My granddaughter loves the movie "The Wizard of Oz". The best part of the movie is when the curtain is pulled back and the real true wizard is exposed. The wizard was just an ordinary man pulling a lot of levers creating smoke and noise. It is now time to pull back the curtain of life and see who has been pulling the levers that created our fears. Let me start off by saying, there is no right or wrong, there are only rules. Ok, you think I am nuts. Let me explain. If you do something wrong, are you not breaking a rule? Think about it? If

you drive over the speed limit, are you not breaking a law? Rule is called the speed limit. It you sin, are you not breaking a rule? It is called the commandments.

When I worked for a large company, we had a book called RSP "Rule of Standard Practice". The book was a foot thick. It was a rule book. Every set of rules has a book. If do not believe me, walk into a law office library.

Let me pull back the curtain. Only people make the rules that determine right and wrong. Instead of being one old man behind a curtain, it is a bunch of old people that set the rules. Do you see where I am going with this concept?

So here is how it works. Let us take the law for example. Someone makes the law, the congress. Someone obeys the law, YOU. Someone enforces the law, police. Someone interrupts the law, judges. Someone punishes us for breaking the law, the penal system.

Whoever thought up this idea should be given the Nobel peace prize. What an ingenious idea. Make a rule, enforce the rule and if you do not follow the rule, create a punishment. In other words, create a fear to control. It does not matter if the rule is right or wrong, it is a rule. Law makers can change the rule anytime. So, what is right or wrong if the rules keep changing.

Here is a thought off the path. For all you folks out there that believe you live in a democracy, you do not. You live in a republic. You do not make the laws; you elect other people to do it for you. Once into office, these law makers can do whatever they want. Most of the time they make the laws for their own personal gain and not your wellbeing. If they do pass a law for your benefit, it is because they are AFRAIRD you will not vote for them.

Ok, let us get back on track. Other than the law of nature, life can be broken down into four sets of rules and nothing else. As soon as you are born, you start your training. They are laws, morals, etiquette, and ethics. Government makes the laws. The church makes sets the morals. Society makes up etiquette. Business creates ethics.

Each of these groups have set punishment if you do not obey their rules. Without punishment there is no fear. Without fear, no one will obey t h e rules. If you break the law, you will lose your freedom in prison. If you break the rules of morals, you could face eternal pain through damnation. If you break the rules of etiquette, you will be rejected by being rejected and shunned. If you break the rules of ethics you will lose your income by being fired.

You live with controlling fear every day. At night you set your alarm so you will not be late for work. Being late for work without a real excuse, will get you fired. You take a shower so you will not smell and be rejected by fellow employees.

You put on the proper cloths so you will fit in. You get in your car and follow the speed limit, so you will not be arrested. O 'yes, guys, did you put the toilet seat down this morning, so your wife does not get upset? Fear – fear – fear and more fear. So, you do not think you are being controlled by fear?

List of Fears

If other know your fears, they will control you. Get help and get rid of your fears or you will spend your life in a cage. Which fears do you have?

Ablutophobia - washing or bathing.
Acrophobia - itching caused by insects.
Acrophobia - sourness.
Achluophobia - darkness. Acoustic phobia - noise.
Acrophobia - heights.
Aerophobia - drafts, air swallowing, or airborne noxious substances. Aeroacrophobia - open high places.
Agateophobia - insanity.
Agliophobia - pain.
Agoraphobia - open spaces or of being in crowded, public places like markets. Fear of leaving a safe place.
Agoraphobia - sexual abuse. Agrizoophobia - wild animals.
Agoraphobia - streets or crossing the street.
Aichmophobia - needles or pointed objects.
Ailurophobia - cats.
Albuminurophobia - kidney disease. Alektorophobia - chickens.
Algophobia - pain. Alliumphobia - garlic.
Allodoxaphobia - opinions. Altophobia - heights.
Amathophobia - dust. Amaxophobia - riding in a car.

Aulophobia - walking.
Maniaphobia - amnesia.
Amychophobia - scratches or being scratched.
Ebolaphobia - looking up.
Acrophobia - wind. (Anemophobia) Androphobia - men.
Anemophobia - air drafts or wind. (Acrophobia)
Anginophobia - angina, choking or narrowness.
Anglophobia - England or English culture, etc.
Agoraphobia - anger or of becoming angry.
Anglophobia - immobility of a joint. Androphobia or Anthophobia - flowers. Anthropophobia - people or society.
Antlophobia - floods. Autophobia - staying single.
Apeirophobia - infinity.
Apiphobia - bees.
Apotemnophobia - persons with amputations.
Arachibutyrophobia - peanut butter sticking to the roof of the mouth.
Arachnophobia or Arachnophobia - spiders.
Aichmophobia - numbers.
Armenophobia - men.
Arson phobia - fire.
Asthenophobia - fainting or weakness.
Astraphobia or Astraphobia - thunder and lightning. (Keraunophobia, Keraunophobia) Astrophobia - stars or celestial space.
Asymmetriphobia - asymmetrical things.
Amaxophobia - ataxia. (muscular incoordination)
Amaxophobia - disorder or untidiness.
Atelophobia - imperfection. Ate phobia - ruin or ruins.
Athazagoraphobia - being forgotten or ignored or forgetting. Automysophobia - atomic explosions.
Amychophobia - failure. Aulophobia - flutes.

Aerophobia - gold. Aurora phobia - Northern lights.
Automysophobia - one that has a vile odor.
Automatonophobia - ventriloquist's dummies, animatronic creatures, wax statues - anything that falsely represents a sentient being.
Automysophobia - being dirty. Autophobia - being alone or of oneself. Aviophobia or Aviophobia - flying.
Bacillophobia - microbes. Bacteriophobia - bacteria.
Halitophobia - missiles or bullets. Oleophobic - Bolsheviks.
Batophobia - gravity.
Basophobia or Basophobia- Inability to stand. Fear of walking or falling. Bathophobia - stairs or steep slopes.
Bathophobia - depth.
Batophobia - heights or being close to high buildings.
Batrachophobia - amphibians, such as frogs, newts, salamanders, etc. Belonephobia - pins and needles. (Aichmophobia)
Bibliophobia - books.
Clinophobia - slime.
Bogy phobia - bogeys or the bogeyman. Botanophobia - plants.
Brontophobia - thunder and lightning.
Belonephobia - toads.
Cacophobia - ugliness.
Cainophobia or Cainotophobia - newness, novelty.
Caligynephobia - beautiful women. Cancerphobia or Carcinophobia - cancer. Cardiophobia - the heart.
Cainophobia - meat. Catagelophobia - being ridiculed.
Canadaphobia - jumping from high and low places.
Bathophobia - sitting.
Catoptrophobia - mirrors.
Cynophobia or Centrophobia - new things or ideas.
Keraunophobia or Keraunophobia - thunder and

lightning. (Astraphobia, Astraphobia) Chaetophobia - hair.

Chemophobia or Chrematophobia - cold. (Frigophobia, Psychophobia) Chemophobia - chemicals or working with chemicals.

Chemophobia - gaiety. Chronophobia - snow.

Herpetophobia - being touched. Chemophobia - hands. Chi optophobia - bats.

Choler phobia - anger or the fear of cholera. Choro phobia - dancing.

Chrematophobia or Chrematophobia - money.

Chromophobia or Chrematophobia - colors.

Chronophobia - time. Coimetrophobia - clocks.

Cacophobia - food. (Sinophobia, Siti phobia)

Claustrophobia - confined spaces.

Cleithrophobe or Cisphobia - being locked in an enclosed place. Kleptophobia - stealing.

Climacophobia - stairs, climbing, or of falling downstairs. Clinophobia - going to bed.

Cleithrophobe or Cleithrophobe - being enclosed. Acidophobia - stings.

Coimetrophobia - comets. Coimetrophobia - cemeteries. Octophobia - coitus.

constipation. Coprophagia - feces.

Counterphobia- The preference by a phobic for fearful situations. Chemophobia - precipices.

Chrysophobia - extreme cold, ice or frost.

Cyberphobia - computers or working on a computer. Cyclophoria - bicycles.

Cymrophobia or Kynophobia - waves or wave like motions. Cynophobia - dogs or rabies.

Cyprid phobia or Cypriphobia or Cyprian phobia or Cyprinophobia - prostitutes or venereal disease.

Dinophobia - dining or dinner conversations.

Emetophobia - insanity.
DE monophobia or Daemonophobia - demons. Demo phobia - crowds. (Agoraphobia) Dendrophilia - trees.
Dental phobia - dentists. Hematophobia - skin lesions. Dermatopathophobia - skin disease.
Centrophobia - objects at the right side of the body.
Iatrophobia - diabetes. Didaskaleinophobia - going to school. Dikephobia - justice.
Dinophobia - dizziness or whirlpools. Diplopodia - double vision.
Dips phobia - drinking.
Dishabiliophobia - undressing in front of someone.
Disposophobia - throwing stuff out. Hoarding.
Domatophobia - houses or being in a house. (Ecophobia, Oikophobia) Doraphobia - fur or skins of animals.
Doxophobia - expressing opinions or of receiving praise. Romaphobia - crossing streets.
Dutch phobia - the Dutch. Dysmorphophobia - deformity.
Dystychiphobia - accidents. Ecclesiophobia -church. Ecophobia - home.
Ecophobia - home surroundings. (Romanophobia, Oikophobia) Eisoptrophobia - mirrors or of seeing oneself in a mirror.
Electrophobia - electricity. Eleutherophobia - freedom.
Europhobia - cats. (Ailurophobia) Emetophobia - vomiting.
Enetophobia - pins. Ochlophobia - crowds.
Enosiophobia or Enissophobia - having committed an unpardonable sin or of criticism. Entomophobia - insects.
Eosophobia - dawn or daylight. Ephebiphobia - teenagers.

Epistaxiophobia - nosebleeds.
Epistemophobia - knowledge. Equinophobia - horses.
Eremophobia - being oneself or of lonliness.
Ereuthrophobia - blushing.
Ergasiophobia- 1) Fear of work or functioning. 2)
Surgeon's fear of operating. Ergophobia - work.
Erotophobia - sexual love or sexual questions.
Euphobia - hearing good news.
Eurotophobia - female genitalia.
Erythrophobia or Erytophobia or Ereuthophobia- 1)
Fear of redlights. 2) Blushing. 3) Red.Febriphobia or
Fibriphobia or Fibriophobia - fever.
Felinophobia - cats. (Ailurophobia, Elurophobia,
Galeophobia, Gatophobia) Francophobia - France or
French culture. (Gallophobia, Galiophobia)
Frigophobia - cold or cold things. (Cheimaphobia,
Cheimatophobia, Psychrophobia) Galeophobia or
Gatophobia - cats.
Gallophobia or Galiophobia- Fear France or French
culture. (Francophobia) Gamophobia - marriage.
Geliophobia - laughter. Gelotophobia - being laughed
at. Geniophobia - chins.
Genophobia - sex.
Genuphobia - knees.
Gephyrophobia or Gephydrophobia or Gephysrophobia
- crossing bridges. Germanophobia - Germany or
German culture.
Gerascophobia - growing old.
Gerontophobia - old people or of growing old.
Geumaphobia or Geumophobia - taste.
Glossophobia - speaking in public or of trying to
speak. Gnosiophobia - knowledge.
Graphophobia - writing or handwriting. Gymnophobia
- nudity.

Gynephobia or Gynophobia - women. Hadephobia - hell.

Hagiophobia - saints or holy things. Hamartophobia - sinning.

Haphephobia or Haptephobia - being touched.

Harpaxophobia - being robbed.

Hedonophobia - feeling pleasure. Heliophobia - the sun.

Hellenologophobia - Greek terms or complex scientific terminology. Helminthophobia - being infested with worms.

Hemophobia or Hemaphobia or Hematophobia - blood.

Heresyphobia or Hereiophobia - challenges to official doctrine or of radical deviation. Herpetophobia - reptiles or creepy, crawly things.

Heterophobia - the opposite sex. (Sexophobia)

Hexakosioihexekontahexaphobia - the number 666.

Hierophobia - priests or sacred things.

Hippophobia - horses.

Hippopotomonstrosesquipedaliophobia - long words.

Hobophobia - bums or beggars.

Hodophobia - road travel. Hormephobia - shock.

Homichlophobia - fog. Homilophobia - sermons.

Hominophobia - men.

Homophobia - sameness, monotony or of homosexuality or of becoming homosexual.

Hoplophobia - firearms.

Hydrargyophobia - mercurial medicines. Hydrophobia - water or of rabies.

Hydrophobophobia - rabies. Hyelophobia or Hyalophobia - glass.

Hygrophobia - liquids, dampness, or moisture.

Hylephobia - materialism or the fear of epilepsy.

Hylophobia - forests.

Hypengyophobia or Hypegiaphobia - responsibility.
Hypnophobia - sleep or of being hypnotized.
Hypsiphobia - height. Iatrophobia - going to the doctor
or of doctors.
Ichthyophobia - fish.
Ideophobia - ideas.
Illyngophobia - vertigo or feeling dizzy when looking
down. Iophobia - poison.
Insectophobia - insects. Isolophobia - solitude, being
alone.
Isopterophobia - termites, insects that eat wood.
Ithyphallophobia - seeing, thinking about, or having an
erect penis.
Japanophobia - Japanese. Judeophobia - Jews.
Kainolophobia or Kainophobia - anything new,
novelty. Kakorrhaphiophobia - failure or defeat.
Katagelophobia - ridicule. Kathisophobia - sitting
down. Katsaridaphobia - cockroaches. Kenophobia -
voids or empty spaces.
Keraunophobia or Ceraunophobia - thunder and
lightning. (Astraphobia, Astrapophobia)
Kinetophobia or Kinesophobia - movement or motion.
Kleptophobia - stealing.
Koinoniphobia - rooms.
Kolpophobia - genitals, particularly female.
Kopophobia - fatigue.
Koniophobia - dust. (Amathophobia) Kosmikophobia -
cosmic phenomenon. Kymophobia - waves.
(Cymophobia) Kynophobia - rabies.
Kyphophobia - stooping.
Lachanophobia - vegetables. Laliophobia or
Lalophobia - speaking. Leprophobia or Lepraphobia -
leprosy. Leukophobia - the color white.
Levophobia - things to the left side of the body.

Ligyrophobia - loud noises.

Lilapsophobia - tornadoes and hurricanes.

Limnophobia - lakes.

Linonophobia - string. Liticaphobia - lawsuits.

Lockiophobia - childbirth.

Logizomechanophobia - computers. Logophobia - words.

Luiphobia - lues, syphillis. Lutraphobia - otters.

Lygophobia - darkness.

Lyssophobia - rabies or of becoming mad.

Macrophobia - long waits.

Mageirocophobia - cooking. Maieusiophobia - childbirth.

Malaxophobia - love play. (Sarmassophobia)

Maniaphobia - insanity.

Mastigophobia - punishment. Mechanophobia - machines. Medomalacuphobia - losing an erection.

Medorthophobia - an erect penis.

Megalophobia - large things. Melissophobia - bees.

Melanophobia - the color black. Melophobia- Fear or hatred of music. Meningitophobia - brain disease.

Menophobia - menstruation. Merinthophobia - being bound or tied up. Metallophobia - metal.

Metathesiophobia - changes.

Meteorophobia - meteors. Methyphobia - alcohol.

Metrophobia- Fear or hatred of poetry. Microbiophobia - microbes. (Bacillophobia) Microphobia - small things.

Misophobia or Mysophobia - being contaminated with dirt or germs. Mnemophobia - memories.

Molysmophobia or Molysomophobia - dirt or contamination. Monophobia - solitude or being alone.

Monopathophobia - definite disease. Motorphobia - automobiles.

Mottephobia - moths.
Musophobia or Muriphobia - mice. Mycophobia- Fear or aversion to mushrooms. Mycrophobia - small things. Myctophobia - darkness. Myrmecophobia - ants. Mythophobia - myths or stories or false statements. Myxophobia - slime. (Blennophobia)Necrophobia - death or dead things. Nebulaphobia - fog. (Homichlophobia)
Nelophobia - glass. Neopharmaphobia - new drugs. Neophobia - anything new.
Nephophobia - clouds. Noctiphobia - the night. Nomatophobia - names. Nosocomephobia - hospitals. Nosophobia or Nosemaphobia - becoming ill. Nostophobia - returning home.
Novercaphobia - your stepmother. Nucleomituphobia - nuclear weapons. Nudophobia - nudity. Numerophobia - numbers.
Nyctohylophobia - dark wooded areas or of forests at night Nyctophobia - the dark or of night.
Obesophobia - gaining weight. (Pocrescophobia) Ochlophobia - crowds or mobs.
Ochophobia - vehicles. Octophobia - the figure 8. Odontophobia - teeth or dental surgery. Odynophobia or Odynephobia - pain. (Algophobia) Oenophobia - wines.
Oikophobia - home surroundings, house. (Domatophobia, Eicophobia) Olfactophobia - smells. Ombrophobia - rain or of being rained on. Ommetaphobia or Ommatophobia - eyes. Omphalophobia - belly buttons.
Oneirophobia - dreams. Oneirogmophobia - wet dreams.
Onomatophobia - hearing a certain word or of names. Ophidiophobia - snakes. (Snakephobia)

Ophthalmophobia - being stared at.

Opiophobia- Fear medical doctors experience of prescribing needed pain medications for patients.

Optophobia - opening one's eyes. Ornithophobia - birds.

Orthophobia - property.

Osmophobia or Osphresiophobia - smells or odors.

Ostraconophobia - shellfish.

Ouranophobia or Uranophobia - heaven.

Pagophobia - ice or frost. Panthophobia - suffering and disease.

Panophobia or Pantophobia - everything. Papaphobia - the Pope.

Papyrophobia - paper.

Paralipophobia - neglecting duty or responsibility.

Paraphobia - sexual perversion.

Parasitophobia - parasites. Paraskavedekatriaphobia - Friday the 13th. Parthenophobia - virgins or young girls.

Pathophobia - disease. Patroiophobia - heredity.

Parturiphobia - childbirth.

Peccatophobia - sinning or imaginary crimes.

Pediculophobia - lice.

Pediophobia - dolls. Pedophobia - children.

Peladophobia - bald people. Pellagrophobia - pellagra.

Peniaphobia - poverty.

Pentheraphobia - mother-in-law. (Novercaphobia)

Phagophobia - swallowing or of eating or of being eaten. Phalacrophobia - becoming bald.

Phallophobia - a penis, esp erect. Pharmacophobia - taking medicine. Phasmophobia - ghosts.

Phengophobia - daylight or sunshine. Philemaphobia or Philematophobia - kissing. Philophobia - falling in love or being in love. Philosophobia - philosophy.

Phobophobia - phobias. Photoaugliaphobia - glaring lights. Photophobia - light.

Phonophobia - noises or voices or one's own voice; of telephones. Phronemophobia - thinking.

Phthiriophobia - lice. (Pediculophobia) Phthisiophobia - tuberculosis.

Placophobia - tombstones. Plutophobia - wealth.

Pluviophobia - rain or of being rained on.

Pneumatiphobia - spirits.

Pnigophobia or Pnigerophobia - choking of being smothered. Pocrescophobia - gaining weight. (Obesophobia) Pogonophobia - beards.

Poliosophobia - contracting poliomyelitis.

Politicophobia- Fear or abnormal dislike of politicians. Polyphobia - many things.

Poinephobia - punishment. Ponophobia - overworking or of pain. Porphyrophobia - purple.

Potamophobia - rivers or running water. Potophobia - alcohol.

Pharmacophobia - drugs. Proctophobia - rectums.

Prosophobia - progress. Psellismophobia - stuttering. Psychophobia - mind.

Psychrophobia - cold. Pteromerhanophobia - flying.

Pteronophobia - being tickled by feathers. Pupaphobia - puppets.

Pyrexiophobia - Fever.

Pyrophobia - fire.

Radiophobia - radiation, x-rays. Ranidaphobia - frogs.

Rectophobia - rectum or rectal diseases.

Rhabdophobia - being severely punished or beaten by a rod, or of being severely criticized. Also fear of magic. (wand)

Rhypophobia - defecation. Rhytiphobia - getting wrinkles. Rupophobia - dirt.

Russophobia - Russians.

Samhainophobia: Fear of Halloween. Sarmassophobia - love play. (Malaxophobia)

Satanophobia - Satan. Scabiophobia - scabies.

Scatophobia - fecal matter. Scelerophibia - bad men, burglars. Sciophobia Sciaphobia - shadows.

Scoleciphobia - worms.

Scolionophobia - school.

Scopophobia or Scoptophobia - being seen or stared at.

Scotomaphobia - blindness in visual field.

Scotophobia - darkness. (Achluophobia) Scriptophobia - writing in public.

Selachophobia - sharks. Selaphobia - light flashes.

Selenophobia - the moon. Seplophobia - decaying matter. Sesquipedalophobia - long words.

Sexophobia - the opposite sex. (Heterophobia)

Siderodromophobia - trains, railroads, or train travel.

Siderophobia - stars.

Sinistrophobia - things to the left or left-handed.

Sinophobia - Chinese, Chinese culture.

Sitophobia or Sitiophobia - food or eating.

(Cibophobia) Snakephobia - snakes. (Ophidiophobia)

Soceraphobia - parents-in-law.

Social Phobia - being evaluated negatively in social situations. Sociophobia - society or people in general.

Somniphobia - sleep. Sophophobia - learning.

Soteriophobia - dependence on others. Spacephobia - outer space.

Spectrophobia - specters or ghosts. Spermatophobia or Spermophobia - germs. Spheksophobia - wasps.

Stasibasiphobia or Stasiphobia - standing or walking. (Ambulophobia) Staurophobia - crosses or the crucifix.

Stenophobia - narrow things or places. Stygiophobia or Stigiophobia - hell.

Suriphobia - mice. Symbolophobia - symbolism. Symmetrophobia - symmetry. Syngenesophobia - relatives. Syphilophobia - syphilis.

Tachophobia - speed.

Taeniophobia or Teniophobia - tapeworms.

Taphephobia Taphophobia - being buried alive or of cemeteries. Tapinophobia - being contagious.

Taurophobia - bulls. Technophobia - technology.

Teleophobia- 1) Fear of definite plans. 2) Religious ceremony. Telephonophobia - telephones.

Teratophobia - bearing a deformed child or fear of monsters or deformed people. Testophobia - taking tests.

Tetanophobia - lockjaw, tetanus. Teutophobia - German or German things. Textophobia - certain fabrics.

Thaasophobia - sitting. Thalassophobia - the sea. Thanatophobia or Thantophobia - death or dying. Theatrophobia - theatres.

Theologicophobia - theology. Theophobia - gods or religion. Thermophobia - heat.

Tocophobia - pregnancy or childbirth. Tomophobia - surgical operations.

Tonitrophobia - thunder.

Topophobia - certain places or situations, such as stage fright.

Toxiphobia or Toxophobia or Toxicophobia - poison or of being accidently poisoned. Traumatophobia - injury.

Tremophobia - trembling. Trichinophobia - trichinosis. Trichopathophobia or Trichophobia - hair.

(Chaetophobia, Hypertrichophobia) Triskaidekaphobia - the number 13.

Tropophobia - moving or making changes.

Trypanophobia - injections.

Tuberculophobia - tuberculosis. Tyrannophobia - tyrants.

Uranophobia or Ouranophobia - heaven. Urophobia - urine or urinating.

Vaccinophobia - vaccination. Venustraphobia - beautiful women. Verbophobia - words.

Verminophobia - germs. Vestiphobia - clothing.

Virginitiphobia - rape.

Vitricophobia - stepfather.

Walloonphobia - the Walloons. Wiccaphobia: Fear of witches and witchcraft.

Xanthophobia - yellow or the word yellow.

Xenoglossophobia - foreign languages.

Xenophobia - strangers or foreigners.

Xerophobia - dryness.

Xylophobia- 1) Fear of wooden objects. 2) Forests.

Xyrophobia-Fear of razors.

Zelophobia - jealousy. Zeusophobia - God or gods.

Zemmiphobia - the great mole rat. Zoophobia - ani

THE END

www.ingramcontent.com/pod-product-compliance
Lightning Source LLC
Chambersburg PA
CBHW072152230526
45467CB00042B/1731